First Facts®

WHAT'S YOUR SOURCE?

USING SOURCES IN YOUR WRITING

BRIEN J JENNINGS

raintree

a Capstone company — publishers for children

Raintree is an imprint of Capstone Global Library Limited, a company incorporated in England and Wales having its registered office at 264 Banbury Road, Oxford, OX2 7DY – Registered company number: 6695582

www.raintree.co.uk
myorders@raintree.co.uk

ISBN 978 1 4747 5439 2
22 21 20 19 18
10 9 8 7 6 5 4 3 2 1

Editorial credits:
Erika L. Shores, editor; Juliette Peters, designer;
Morgan Walters, media researcher; Kathy McColley, production specialist
Printed and bound in India

Photo credits:
Alamy: Sean Prior, 21; Capstone Studio: Karon Dubke, bottom 17, middle 17; Shutterstock: Artur. B, (icons) design element, David Osborn, (penguin) Cover, imtmphoto, (girls) Cover, Maksim Kabakou, bottom 11, mattomedia Werbeagentur, 15, Orange Line Media, 13, Rawpixel.com, 5, 7, top 11, Shahrul Azman, 19, Supphachai Salaeman, design element throughout, Tonis Pan, (computer) Cover, Tyler Olson, 9, Vladimir Volodin, 12, wavebreakmedia, 17

British Library Cataloguing in Publication Data
A full catalogue record for this book is available from the British Library.

Every effort has been made to contact copyright holders of material reproduced in this book. Any omissions will be rectified in subsequent printings if notice is given to the publisher.

All the Internet addresses (URLs) given in this book were valid at the time of going to press. However, due to the dynamic nature of the Internet, some addresses may have changed, or sites may have changed or ceased to exist since publication. While the author and publisher regret any inconvenience this may cause readers, no responsibility for any such changes can be accepted by either the author or the publisher.

Contents

All about sources

A library is full of sources. Books, newspapers, websites and videos are common sources. A librarian can help you find the right source for information on your topic.

> **TIP!** Encyclopedias can be great sources to get started with research. Most encyclopedias are online and easy to search. Encyclopedias give facts on many different topics.

The internet makes it easy to find information. Anyone can go online almost anywhere and find almost anything. You need to be careful to make sure the information you find online is true. Look for websites created by museums, universities and news organizations. People who work for these places make sure the information they put on their websites is true.

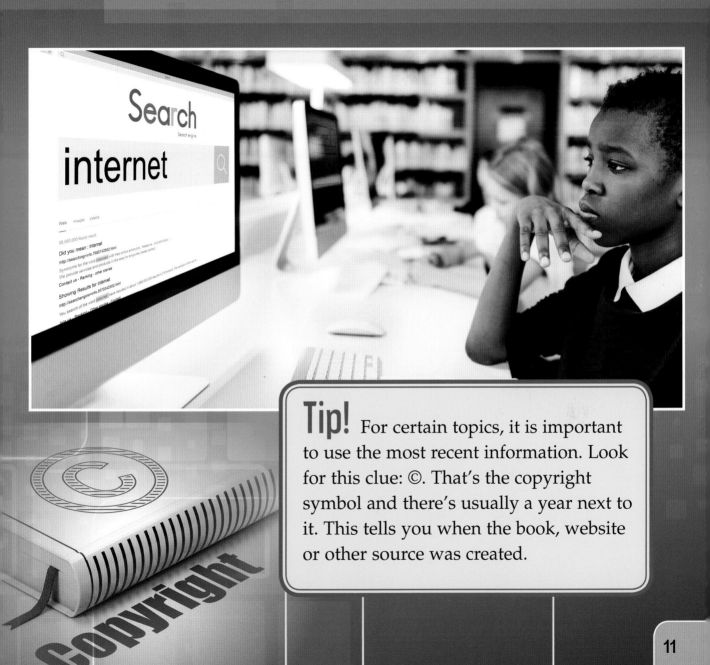

Tip! For certain topics, it is important to use the most recent information. Look for this clue: ©. That's the copyright symbol and there's usually a year next to it. This tells you when the book, website or other source was created.

Go right to the source

Using **primary** sources in your research is a great idea. Photos and letters are primary sources. Diaries and **interviews** are primary sources too. They are made by people who have first-hand experience of an event. People wrote down their experiences or took photos.

primary first
interview meeting
    to ask someone
    questions to find out
    more about something

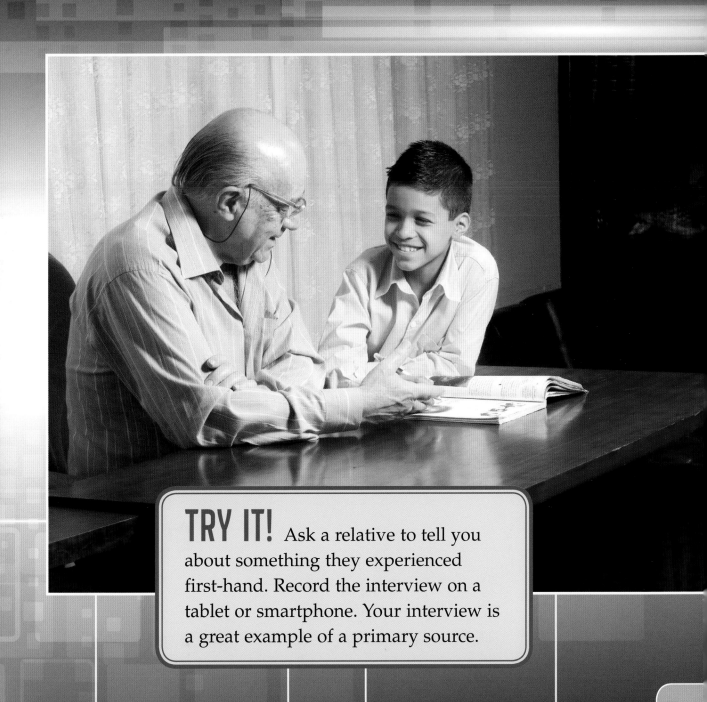

TRY IT! Ask a relative to tell you about something they experienced first-hand. Record the interview on a tablet or smartphone. Your interview is a great example of a primary source.

Choosing sources

With so many sources to choose from, picking the right ones is an important step in research. Ask some questions to find out whether a source is useful. Is there enough information, and is it easy to understand? Is the source **trustworthy**? Can you find the author and **publisher** information? Does the source contain facts or opinions?

TIP! If you are unsure about what source to use, ask a librarian or teacher. Librarians and teachers know what makes a good source.

trustworthy something you can believe in
publisher person or company who makes media
available to the public

Copyright and plagiarism

The copyright symbol does more than show how old a source is. It also lets you know that someone owns the content of the source. Authors, photographers and illustrators often own their own work. Sometimes publishers pay for the right to own this work.

Deserts are *ecosystems*.
These areas are dry and get little rain. Most deserts are very hot, but some are cold. Some deserts even get snow. Some deserts are sandy, while others are rocky.

What Are They? | Where Are They? | Desert Plants | Desert Animals | Spreading Deserts

Print

Teacher Resources
© 2017 Capstone

capstone

Raintree is an imprint of Capstone Global Library Limited, a company incorporated in England and Wales having its registered office at 264 Banbury Road, Oxford, OX2 7DY – Registered company number: 6695582

www.raintree.co.uk
myorders@raintree.co.uk

Text © Capstone Global Library Limited 2017
The moral rights of the proprietor have been asserted.

Editorial Credits
Carrie Braulick Sheely, editor; Juliette Peters, designer; Wanda Winch, media researcher; Tori Abraham, production specialist

ISBN 978-1-4747-2505-7
20 19 18 17 16
10 9 8 7 6 5 4 3 2 1

British Library Cataloguing in Publication Data
A full catalogue record for this book is available from the British Library.

Acknowledgements
We would like to thank the following for permission to reproduce photographs:
Ardea.com: Steve Hopkin, 11; Dreamstime: Bereta, 9, Laozhang, 19, Nancykennedy, 15; Shutterstock: Andre Mueller, 17, Bachkova Natalia, 22, Dennis van de Water, 7, Evgeniya Tiphyashina, cover, 5, Henrik Larsson, 13, icarmen13, 1, Igor Sokolov (breeze), back cover, Jan Miko, 21, LianeM, daisy background used throughout book, Maxal Tamor, 20, Oleksandr Kozachenko, 6, picsfive, note design, Valentina Proskurina, back cover (ladybug), 3 (all), 24

Every effort has been made to contact copyright holders of material reproduced in this book. Any omissions will be rectified in subsequent printings if notice is given to the publisher.

All the Internet addresses (URLs) given in this book were valid at the time of going to press. However, due to the dynamic nature of the Internet, some addresses may have changed, or sites may have changed or ceased to exist since publication. While the author and publisher regret any inconvenience this may cause readers, no responsibility for any such changes can be accepted by either the author or the publisher.

Contents

When writing a report, you should not copy words directly from sources. Using other people's words as your own is called **plagiarism**. It is the same as stealing someone else's work.

TIP! Don't copy word for word. Only write the most important words. These are called **keywords**. Make sure you write down where you find your information.

plagiarism using someone else's words, pictures, sounds or ideas without permission or giving them credit

You've found the best sources. You've gathered the information. You've made a list of the titles and authors of your sources. Now it's time to write your research report.

Be an information detective to find and use the best sources.

Ask yourself these questions:
- How up-to-date is the information?
- Does your source have information you can use?
- Can you tell who created the source? Who is the author or publisher?
- Is your source full of facts or opinions?
- If it is a website, are there ads? Is the website trying to sell you something? If it is, you might not trust it.

Glossary

accurate   exactly correct

interview   meeting to ask someone questions to find out more about something

keyword   important word

non-fiction   written works about real people, places, objects or events

opinion   way of thinking about something, not a fact

plagiarism   using someone else's words, pictures, sounds or ideas without permission or giving them credit

primary   first

publisher person or company that makes media available to the public

research   study and learn about a topic

trustworthy   something you can believe in

Books

I Can Write Reports (I Can Write), Anita Ganeri (Raintree, 2013)

Learning About Primary Sources (Media Literacy for Kids), Nikki Bruno Clapper (Raintree, 2015)

What is Informational Writing? (Connect with Text), Charlotte Guillain (Raintree, 2015)

Websites

www.bbc.co.uk/bitesize/ks2/english/writing/newspapers/read/1/
Learn more about the parts of a non-fiction text, and how to write a news report.

www.bbc.co.uk/newsround
The BBC newsround website is a great place to start if you are writing a report about a news event.

Comprehension questions

1. What is one way you can decide if a source is trustworthy?

2. What does plagiarism mean?

3. Describe why primary sources are useful in your research.

Index